It Must Be New Zealand

Fay Looney

NEW
HOLLAND

My day begins at first light wherever I am and whatever the weather, and the rewards more than compensate the effort. More often than not I will be on a beach or bush track, rather than a mountain, these days. But Mt Taranaki – just outside my back door – continues to inspire my work and has taught me much about changing light and spectacular moments.

The landscape shapes our lives where we work and play. I am sure, though, that some work is in fact play, and this is reflected in the characters I meet and who turn up in the images within this book: Chaddy the storyteller and his English lifeboat, Fleur and her unique restaurant on the wharf at Moeraki, fishermen we meet on lakes and rivers, farmers and families in remote and beautiful places.

People who look at my images tend to say I must be patient, but as my family will confirm, I am anything but. So it is the spontaneous moments I capture as I travel, such as the dolphins that hurled themselves into the sky behind a small yellow dinghy unnoticed by the occupant, who simply kept fishing. I captioned the shot 'It must be New Zealand', and that was the beginning of a whole new journey.

My journeys are seldom alone these days, so thank you, my family and friends, for the company and the helping hand.

This book is for Harry Jnr., Mack, Kate, Ben and Sam.

Fay Looney

It must be New Zealand ...

Owae Marae, Waitara, Taranaki

Where a culture of welcome awaits.

Moeraki holiday camp, North Otago

Where first light promises new surprises ...

Fleur Sullivan gathers bull kelp for her restaurant kitchen, Moeraki

and culinary treats outside the door.

Eastbourne, Wellington

Where the morning sun lights up distant peaks ...

Central Wellington

or skyscrapers.

Whakarewarewa, Rotorua

Where a spa can take up the whole backyard ...

Hot Water Beach, Coromandel Peninsula

or a beach.

Cooks Beach, Coromandel Peninsula

Where tractors get the best view ...

Papaaroha Beach, Coromandel Peninsula

but come with terms and conditions.

Esk Valley, Napier

Where seasons bring colour and fragrance ...

New Zealand pigeon (kereru) eating berries of nikau palm

and delicacies for birds.

Where old traditions ...

Julie Kipa Moko artist at work

create new art.

Port Jackson, Coromandel Peninsula

Where you can take a holiday with your horse ...

and cool off.

Sandy Bay, Coromandel Peninsula

Akaroa, Banks Peninsula

Where transportation is eclectic ...

and inventive.

Top-dressing, Taranaki

Where work is rewarded with breathtaking views ...

Manaia, Taranaki

and small towns are rewarded with success.

Anzac Day, New Plymouth, Taranaki

Where we are grateful to those who have died for our peace ...

Waimea, Nelson

and for our peaceful places.

Oparara track, Kahurangi National Park

Where the emerald of the bush ...

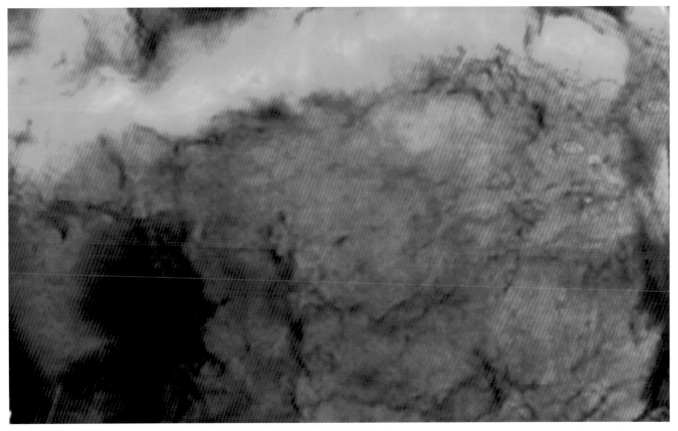

Pounamu (greenstone)

is matched by the rock lying within.

Hops, Motueka, Nelson

Where it's a short journey from field ...

Vulcan Hotel, St Bathans, Otago

to pint glass.

Strathmore, Taranaki

Where if you work hard ...

Port Jackson, Coromandel Peninsula

you ride home with the boss.

North Beach, Karamea, Westland

Where mother's milk is precious ...

and the best is saved for the young.

Dolphins, Coromandel Peninsula

Where the sea life is bigger than your boat ...

Waihaha, Lake Taupo

sometimes.

Purangi Reserve, Cooks Beach, Coromandel Peninsula

Where the kids can dig for lunch ...

for Dad to cook.

Blackball Hilton, West Coast

Where old towns are reborn with a twist ...

Coromandel Hotel, Coromandel Township

and hospitality is extended to all.

Raglan, Waikato

Where all directions lead to enchanted places ...

National Park, central North Island

and adventure.

Mokau Beach, Taranaki

Where the steel-blue sea is broken by whitecaps ...

Sperm whale, Kaikoura

and whales.

Cathedral Cove, Coromandel Peninsula

Where around every corner is a film set ...

Near Glenorchy, Lake Wakatipu

in our Middle-earth.

Southern Alps

Where long white clouds follow the land's spine ...

Katiki Beach, Otago

all the way down to the sea.

Lake Taupo

Where still waters ...

Benmore Dam, Canterbury

are a powerful force.

Where art is alive ...

Granity, Westport

Oyster Bay, Otago Peninsula

on the streets.

Lake Taupo

Where you can fish under a rainbow ...

Kuaotunu, Coromandel Peninsula

or swing at the end of the road.

Dusky dolphins, Kaikoura

Where the surf is full ...

Back Beach, New Plymouth

of all sorts of life.

Lake Tekapo, Mackenzie Country

Where sometimes you just need to sit with the view …

St Bathans, Central Otago

or follow it home.

Dunstan, Central Otago

Where the landscape is painted

Akaroa, Banks Peninsula

with beautiful light.

Thames, Coromandel Peninsula

Where you know who's living inside

Granity, Westport

by the details.

Kawarau Gorge, Queenstown

Where you can pay to be petrified ...

Queenstown

and then plan your next adventure.

Hawke's Bay A & P Show

Where everyone is a team supporter ...

Farmland, Waikato

yes, everyone.

'Chaddy', Port Taranaki

Where the waters deliver surprises ...

Whitebaiting, Opotiki, Bay of Plenty

for those with the patience to wait.

Huka Park, Taupo

Where travel is tranquil ...

Huka Jet, Huka Falls, Taupo

or rapid.

Where everything is an inspiration ...

Taranaki Daily News Fashion Art Awards

for art.

Clifton Rugby Club, Taranaki

Where the whole family is involved in the game

Brazilian students, Spotswood College, New Plymouth

and the whole world watches.

Where pavlova is an indisputably Kiwi invention ...

Pohutukawa, New Plymouth

and Christmas trees decorate themselves.

Lake Taupo

Where solitude is immense ...

Lake Taupo

and uninterrupted.

Schoolchildren's tiles, Port of Gisborne

Where children's art colours the landscape ...

Oakura School beach planting project, Taranaki

and kids make sure it's protected.

Albatross

Where instinct brings you home ...

Seaward Kaikoura Range, Kaikoura

to safe and peaceful waters.

Heritage Hotel, Queenstown, Otago

It must be New Zealand.

First published in 2009 by New Holland Publishers (NZ) Ltd
Auckland • Sydney • London • Cape Town

www.newhollandpublishers.co.nz

218 Lake Road, Northcote, Auckland 0627, New Zealand
Unit 1, 66 Gibbes Street, Chatswood, NSW 2067, Australia
86–88 Edgware Road, London W2 2EA, United Kingdom
80 McKenzie Street, Cape Town 8001, South Africa

A catalogue record of this book is available from the National Library of New Zealand

ISBN 978 1 86966 262 2

10 9 8 7 6 5 4 3 2 1

Publishing manager: Matt Turner
Editor: Michele Powles
Design: Fay Looney, Dee Murch
Cover design: Cheryl Rowe

Colour reproduction by Pica Digital Pte Ltd, Singapore
Printed in China by Everbest Printing Co, on paper sourced from sustainable forests

Front cover: Church of the Good Shepherd, Lake Tekapo, Mackenzie County

Title page: Port Jackson road, Coromandel Peninsula